T0284606

TRACER

OMNIDAWN PUBLISHING   RICHMOND, CALIFORNIA   2009

RICHARD **GREENFIELD** *TRACER*

DESIGN AND COMPOSITION BY QUEMADURA

PRINTED OFFSET ON ACID-FREE, RECYCLED PAPER

BY THOMSON-SHORE, INC., DEXTER, MICHIGAN

green
press
INITIATIVE

Omnidawn Publishing is committed to preserving ancient forests and natural resources. We elected to print this title on 30% postconsumer recycled paper, processed chlorine-free. As a result, for this printing, we have saved:

1 Trees (40' tall and 6-8" diameter)
525 Gallons of Wastewater
1 million BTUs of Total Energy
68 Pounds of Solid Waste
127 Pounds of Greenhouse Gases

Omnidawn Publishing made this paper choice because our printer, Thomson-Shore, Inc., is a member of Green Press Initiative, a nonprofit program dedicated to supporting authors, publishers, and suppliers in their efforts to reduce their use of fiber obtained from endangered forests.

For more information, visit www.greenpressinitiative.org

Environmental impact estimates were made using the Environmental Defense Paper Calculator. For more information visit: www.edf.org/papercalculator

LIBRARY OF CONGRESS CATALOGING-IN-PUBLICATION DATA

GREENFIELD, RICHARD, 1969–

TRACER / RICHARD GREENFIELD. — 1ST AMERICAN PBK. ED.

P. CM.

ISBN 978-1-890650-38-4 (PBK. : ACID-FREE PAPER)

I. TITLE.

PS3607.R454T73 2009

811'.6—DC22

2009015639

PUBLISHED BY OMNIDAWN PUBLISHING

RICHMOND, CALIFORNIA WWW.OMNIDAWN.COM

(510) 237-5472 (800) 792-4957

10 9 8 7 6 5 4 3 2 1

I

I

SPEAKING FOR

Open a window:

a colony of winged ants has stained their flightless self to my wall,

collective stake without the propagating sky spreading in my

basement;

above, truer scripts of morning light suffuse into the extremities

of my lot, measuring into the fractured foundation: the ivy

is the new scrawl;

I am a reader there, reading aloud, deploying a plan as a voice as

an imagined moral presence in the listening devices and oscillating

sprinklers that automate into shadows, because

this voice speaks only to itself, makes decisions without

considering others,

　　　　and some decisions cost,

　　　is it ants below worrying me? or the yellow house violated,

the yard's perimeter broken, the coiled hose beneath the useless

rhododendron,

　　　or outward, the controlled sugar maples lining the designed

street, the white alder drift, the T-bar frames of the clothesline with the

floating brisk whites at the dusky end, at the edge of the (lately) garden,

sick husks
　　　　　(my fault);

Already I am we,

    the small rectangles of all of the backyards of all of us, our washed

sidewalks, our sweeper nozzles— our detritus colludes at the ends of

the driveways, the leaves in the neighbor trees glisten, the utilities

hung high in the air between the houses;

Our mail is here,

    I read here too that the corner influence brings up the price,

    that in the State, questions are protected until they are

answered, until we listen and

    turn the noon into an archived document of torture, until falling

    statues precede the capital that permeates after, until our needs are formed behind blast shields and sharpened into form

and played in the role of rage

which I read now is emitted as a remotely-activated hypothesis,

until what could be

terrified could be the embryonic atoms of a greater terror

BASTION

My reach into an unlit hole

transmitted the void through the

whole bulk of my arm— the dead air

around the appendage actually activated

and what was there? an instrument

a valve to turn on or off as the rye weather

turned up, I thought I needed to govern

the understructure of my home, I reached

in an instant for the fact of accounts—

a bit to warm me, to say made it, to say plan kept

Was it merited, with my body stressed

to the floor, stretched for the catch—

extracting nothing? not the fist stopped

in the mouth, the lachrymal emptying

into a blank wall, the ceruse interior

the so-called emanate walking through the

matter of this and obliterating so much

of its shell, wounding others along the way,

using up too much, wasting more—

inscribing one's name in the unfeasible

thrall of the moment, no one is

so real, judgment is its own prison:

now we pay to get into public space;

along the repeating strip out the window,

for every new notion, the detonation of the old;

living alone is thought to be my plan

——maintenance——

if (if only)

by a scrape

RAPIER / RAVINE

I, then we speaks, a collapse, failing to maintain its fiction— in a false

scale of time, the event omitted, rapier in the background, survivor in

the foreground, I then we, but in revolt to the authority of the frame

or the willingness of the viewer to entice us (I/we) outward to

valorize the dialectic in the slash to hear the collective singing,

yesterday, like patriot noise or "gutshot of the horse," "a man in the

ravine rolling" and "weeping" "asking for momma on the ravine,"

"some alive but little left on the ravine," "he got himself up, he did not

know how he got himself up," "soldiers on the ravine found a woman,

she was faking but they made sure and killed her," "they laid down the

beast, it was pretty weak," "many wore shirts emblazoned with

grapeshot," the last report, I, we, the bluestem, grows thick at

massacre park

MAVERICK

At the floating-leaf center

Leaky buckets in the brigade

Now we need a leader

We like a man walking ahead

The scale of that man is correct

He strides in half-prophet mode

Into the blue confusion of a vista

Where whatever the distance of the

Opposite shore

He rounds the lakeshore one foot priestly

The other violator

The depths sound thankless fathoms

Spare small change for the well

Or welfare

SUBLIMITY WILL NOT BE THE END

The latter days exercise beside annihilation

the obese limbs of a plum tree bolt off

blue-tone cloudlets mass over a dry lake

and the cried-out grass of a desert city

is swathed in the fanatic will to be

All actors and spectators age

under the sun,   pass, wither

carry,——   my body is here to

add episode in the soil record

In so fatal, I grow interactive

stave fullness, stop the mouth

suture the stomach, the purity

of the highway halts, bleached line

against the burnt hills— deep object—

the metastatic beg— de facto

humming along

None must wait for contagion

where it is already welcomed—

I open for my consequence

a light melody that brushes up to my stop

and rules the core

contraction where ego no longer

conducts itself but lives quietly

within its new excess

4 July

The daisy cutter elegies flowered in the night, over the very

spot, my friend no longer called, three blocks over on Ogden Street,

a year ago, it was the start of the month, the rent paid, no money left,

the lack was the vest pocket charm saying, "ok, follow the fanfare

home," passing the hollow heart of public art, toward the black

epitaphs of my ancestors, their bones have been the hoax of blood,

they have fallen into false lineage

The city trees were sickly, glossed brilliant from the spraying,

minimalist fruit withered into the limbs, this palled into "it,"

and pollen sublated into it, the animals kept dropping from their

nests, opinion was an inoffensive dissipate in the air

I thought of the parent cells in me, their fight always inflicts debt,

the stylus carved through the soft vinyl, the late hour

resounded with its slowcore charge: neither the atoms, neither

initiator, neither remnant of thought's thought gone and thus

answered—

Was it the syringe in the toilet tank I found near the leak? how many

tenants ago? but once more, the water filled the bowl, something new

added to the list of errands, hearing the demand for the dead's return,

hearing a birthday symphony, a mound crowned, phosphorous stars

spraying over,

no irony

THE SESSION

Began with paper arguments, wipe-away lines crossed at the cardinal x

    of the low table, the surface the oily luster that absorbed the cotton-

colored catalog light, began, actually then, with symmetry;

    the ragged tour entered a hall of empty pedestals, and it was the

end of evolution,

      where the molecule-sized Idea on display rubbed my wallet in

my pocket,

but nothing to spend, and I folded my hand, turned a corner of relics;

then someone wanted to know the "use" of it;

    in the next room, the restored typewriters from the Disaster

tapped atonal measures, they were repeating my initials;

the nudes had lost their vulnerabilities, the blown-blue demeanor

of a basecoat was the only antiphon of these critics;

I could not forget the rescinded offer of their attachment to me,

which hung there also,

and as the session continued, I recognized a thesis, on

daylight, and its twin—

the pay-off,

I asked

what is it, is it affirmation, is decay behind the answer,

a lasting epiphany,

a hot-point revelation, dirty chunks of mortality,

is this for the spectator, admission's fee,

though also the sense that none cares, fine, but there is

this frieze;

I think my moment was in the skylight room,

where, as the speaker's voice caught

on the rear walls and held the treble of the small insight,

the cloud's shadows moved over the center of the audience (I thought)

without relation

VULCAN

At the cataract exit
(one such thought turns once only)

dispel enough

to destroy memory

deadly, the crystals' slow needling ascendance a lifetime before,
without the regress or energy of anyone— now the inflection of
control and self-centeredness, received impressions of the surface
teething the threshold of panic. Little light, the act burgeons from us
a spectacle
tree,
upside down

The mainline of the surface tree
rends toward the interior glow of our fear,
to breach the ceiling of the system—

And it spreads down into the cold
among the stalline stars
as its inverted form

Germinal, a hell flame blazes blonde
and cooks the white meat of a feast

All workers of an unfinished complex
clear sweat from salt

   no longer

   (no longer)

  confirmed by alabaster leaves

  shaking in the hoar-wind abating the light

Started with the stamen—

a fragile scheme

I would

appraise it

I looked at it

The opaque hub of it

resisted

The gaze wormed

itself into the fruit

and turned

to see its source

through the hole

it had chewed

Who builds-over

overwrites

the already-there

pierces ovary

draws kingdom blood

The imperial conceits

begin w/ bouquets

Counting the tapestries—

the ten thousand

spoils secreted

to the casual sea

for a minute

mirrored in the sun

A critique began . . .

Did I pour acid or water?

Counted the very volume

Oil fields on fire

acetated award-winning

This was the

stigma of *irsa*, iris

erased—

the tender style

of the flower

turned financial

HELLFIRE

I want to wrap my

compositional theory in duct tape—

in the new idea, no

fuses, one step removed from

the act, the trace embodies

the pain of pain; narrative

shrapnels into its spectators

the aftermath a red fountain

(post-ethic) font, flashbang of

the untitled, the still unframed

concussion (the firstlight) or

the casting of my soul

into a paradise

The brain is a nest, the eye

is a tiny architecture;

the iris is the eye's theory—

self-deluded but trying to

see the green world burning

in the first freeze, I hear

a choice in the brush,

spaced in the phrases of

the central area in the

lunch hour, the crowd

spills over itself, the flung

scraps became the feeding

indiscretion of dull birds

popping in a brown colorfield

at their feet; election day,

consumption of entirety

in a warble, I

hear a choice in the evening,

and then another brood

the same as before?

huddled on the wire above

the intersection, the lights,

they are mild interest for me

and it is the end of the week,

    they perch with choice and

sweetly bag other songs

.

The pretty violations bleed best in the background,

a strain of blood in every spatter-stroke of the instrument
      at the center, never hampered

by its criticism, though the ear tunes to the string-break of protest—

though cloudy futurity fills in the fires of a date, the date ever
      concealed there,

and thus the magnesium in the flame finds the fine point of its burn,
      so do I

watch now—— through night-vision patina, melee erupts,
      trace the outline, the trace

that is the indicator and the censor and the opening— first
      in the sequence which demarks

elsewhere, by sending out violent tendrils,

the future needs a signature signed out of strife, to take up its space
      on the line; I'm

speaking, and this lease is a promise, and the law is a gesture
      toward action,

but when I leave here I will see the source—
      two vacant rooms, seven bare windows—

incite the questions toward this moving-day, vacancy
      is finally anti-climactic:

I am more than a clouded departure, I detach from my owning,
      the vestige imprints in the carpet,

my occupation lies in the stains, in the in medias res radiance of the
      missing curtains,

the room cleared of the fixtures, cleared of the clutter from old
      rooms, interlocutors between my body

and its incentives, with rot in the air,

with the open wound of leaving in the midst, taking seconds,
      with the dawn's effacing

daylight, the rooms evacuated, loud nailholes in the drywall
      leak autobiography

RECOVERY EFFORT

As one splits distress

one contains it

and paints the target,

the stunned lungs are exposed to the commons, walkways,

the ruins of the neighborhood,

behind this, unapologetic power— call it blight, start over, then do it

again—

the history of the block before detonation will be abbreviated in

the name of its replacement,

we are watching it again

the structure appears to implode, sinking deeper than its stake

in an economy of force, dispersing beyond its matter,

there is no structure, no form, no consistent style, the matter,

dispersed, is not quantifiable: the recovered shoes miss their matches,

the image of fear unfolds approximate to the transecting light,

in the spreading haze,

I think of a ray of a film projector above the crests of chairs in a

theater, the dust particles held in stasis, explosion images,

the audience has been here before, cinema is

eidetic in the moment

and hurts;

Foxes appear in the parking lot—

and first nature moves among the ruins of second nature,

these foxes keen their lungs and their tongues

in the quires, there is disappointment in the dawn,

(the image of foxes is a memento, the height of the autumn)

the film has stopped, but the narrative resumes:

we found the filthy furniture, we were children playing near the

strobing eye of the sun, the toys projected our future, we

plowed our roads and crushed our homes,

each of our toys seeped too early into the earth, the noon rotted in

the flowery scent

of corpse-vapor

THE FUTURE

Terror has its imitations

I go out and cut the flowers

this is an arrangement, too—

I am also subject to

the hysterical point of view

the sunset exposes the matter

on a plain and even the thought

of casting a shadow, my intention

is too much, there is too much

everyday competing splendor

to see how it is posed for the best

effect; in the western trajectory

defeat is a tunnel through a mountain

leading to the indigo snowfields

and their gems underfoot,

to solstice stars, to the last one

standing, to a summit

summited before; access is defeat—

I can stand anywhere; the fear of radicals

burns out of a hole, the objective

ejected into entropy at the saberpoint

on the violet atmosphere, the cold bulbs

remain interred into their beds

we go on, as a guess, interposed

between the private and the republic

by default, we do not want to know

we want our reward; so finally, I

walk the river trail, my leisure earned

the river splits the city: hardly a flow

the fish bones litter the bight, foam

floats by, the end is stuck, in retribution,

in the fall air, half-masts flapping

radiated tips, piano plinks, gray-gray sky

   is useless

        humming, then

the victim names

  or aesthetics—

OUT OF LACK

Careless to invoke it

   but the delusion of voice is not enough

   an aggregate tune stranded

   on the sticky trap of the tongue

   no one is weeping, including me

   not on my street, not where the

   bicycles are locked at the train station

   not where the rooftops teeth into space

   I saw enough people at the park today

   I vacated myself

through the veil

   of the other

   (no nearer to that other)

and a survivor entangled

in a wire

asks for no witness

to this costly crossing;

I want to want company again;

The victim tells a story and they listen,

they applaud; it sounds like a kind of

loneliness, or a cavern, or an unworked funerary slab

denied by the memoirist for the sake of his art;

—   Applause at negative daybreak,

coming out of the meadowland

headlock of pity

the morning-after,

post lyric

o, o

interrupt me—

"

In the interludal breath

prove (again) the night
the southern sun

the frequent breaks
in the background nature noise

getting started

The wall glistens with fresh graffiti but vandals do not extort,

what it says is more tone than message, I've forgotten now

this is here

I'll make one uninvolved observation:
these kids mark their own

stylized record of passing through immutable empty lots,

as the insects flicker in the serial conical amber streetlight, each is a dot against the shift, put on display, a pixel

in the representation

and I want Real time to pass in it

to open with it
to swing on it

or surveil the border city

a porch door opens, the light

a porch door shuts, the light;

kites flee holes along the river (border crossings) within reception of
the

  gray listening stations, downriver the stonebed bleeds fertilizer

into the gulf of wastes,

Who am I against the wall
if not the wall itself?

Is it enough to say there is difference?

  or disproportion at the wall?

(no open gates— wet letters tagging the dawn)

the walls between the haves

& the have-nots

SPECIES

In the fringe month I hear the new wasps hitting the glass

they have come from the white hem of a dead inland sea

a break-through under the sun, an advancing tendril

killing its host in its reach into that

otherness, wearing the breeding scent of the creep

they peak in regional clusters and spring convulsive, all fences

hot integers in the clarity-yellow dotting back to the lapse

SALE

$1.00 each

(2) plastic bangle bracelets; (1) pasta
fork, not used; (Pair) ivory tone semi-
loop earrings w gold tone accents;
(Pair) earrings, silver imbued;
(1) ceramic ginger bread boy pin;
(1) zippered bag clear plastic;
(1) California-style plastic hair
barrette, thin; (2 sets of 2) gold crest
side combs; (1) metallic hair turban,
new in package; (1) extra large all
cotton towel, soft; (1) brand-name
kitchen towel, rough terry; (1) doily,
6 inch square, not used

Refuse of time

It spends

In happiness

And not—

Self-hatred eventually coils upon itself—

the warning rattle is without context, separated from the dead snake

in the path now gone, the rattle snapped off and slid into my pocket,

inutile to the fang;

two years

    living on a road by a square copse of trees, a sloping cattle-

thinned field to the south, a tobacco barn black at the periphery of the

woods, the poplar and basswood and ash stripped of leaves and

the pasture turned tawny in October, the barn roseate in the

afternoons, relapsing into russet in the evening, swallows swung

through the black square of the open loft doors;

some days I walked a narrow dirt path and stared inside at the

empty stalls and the bales of hay;

The acre became an acre only in the moment of its purchase,

the graders cut a road onto the lot, and the upturned red clay

lining lost its intense bleed as it dried,

they leveled the inclines and put down cisterns for the creek to

run under planned parking, they tore out trees by chains,

I knew it would be absorbed into background, it would be our

newest gesture, a nod beside the glossy new, worse, their smiling

recovery, the proof of conscientious capital,

ghost-lining;

I watched the y-wing beams of the loft rip off all together,

refusing to release their hold, it was burned as a whole with the scrap

of the barn in the field in April, the men watched, the skeleton was

dragged and the remnants were burned a little more with fire wands

and whatever remained was buried in a large scrap hole

The dull concords of middle age hang over the site. This thing in my

pocket, I am unable to borrow from my lessons, I want to testify but it

is all description and no reflection . . .

a red field hedges the risk against the paths, the drought-leaves

catch there, black screams of crows circle in the last drolls of smoke,

turning into it, merging with it, for the first time distinguished by it

TACIT RAINBOW

Friend at the end,

I've veered this way with ruinous humility, thrived in this gloom

my only worry in the middle of this playing field, also

a breeding ground

Out in the coppice I butchered together a red bouquet for you

then we hid among the briars and down in the crawl

You looked over my cuts   we played another game

we saw the wasted on the border, grown-up

wraithing before us

Seek no more, but tell me what you saw

said they

we sought to service

A REGIME

First the plural gauze of pleasure

was placed over all of the scene

then I dropped the clothing into

a heap and the wind

pulled the slight flickers

the clearing blinked

in the fire, an early planet

smoldered alone in a hole

in the canopy, I stood there

the proleptic spring

was wet in the ground and unmarked

by the usual green rituals of birth

the crabgrass began

growing lateral beneath the managing blades;

interior poverty had papered the empty drawers

the cleaning rags fueled into the chemical burn

a blue ring kept flaring in the treetops

what was left

was the lemon kitchen
blooded porcelain sink
glass-knobbed doors
miniature gas stove;

the too-early cricket between

the double-panes discharged a

muted strain (I imagined) filling

its own clarion space

none listened

for the enjoyment of listening

was there response in the garden?

was there the assumption

of ascent in this moment?

I remember

after a cabinet council

I lifted the screen and

set the little excess loose to the night

and there was a thought of the

sure assemblage of light there

when the break-in note

signaled from the low lawn

and I was thinking of the lien

the money not there;

a triangle pattern had formed around

the self-consuming beacon, me

the three points absorbed each other,

then I was on a point

inside/outside;

when the dialogue bubble

erupted from my mouth

with excuses,

it stopped itself,

it stopped itself

ANNALS

Here in the outskirts,

where sea fossils
 locked into the ridges,

                    wrote

"The rain sluiced
 the trees bare of the earth—"

          this was my history, too,

       here in the outskirts

    nothing I do is witnessed, nothing I build lasts, I am happy,
    work keeps me going,

I am remote but I know

the old world is still out there, too

where the roads are intraworking,

    the last dust and the vermin slip by, unnamed,

                    here

self-protection is a shutdown of empathy,

I forget friends, the calendar

is a reliable prediction,

the paper that yellows in the oil-light
            on an unmovable table, beneath
            a window faced piper-westward,

my beard is growing now,
            filling up my neck,

skin itchy,

while the dripping faucet
awls a hole into the sink
or the firmament

with well water

or the sun swivels
            around the slow agon of time,
            and bakes its mark into paint...

and I would rather not speak

of my address

or the address of my occupation

both

on roads

named after locals

A SPECTACLE

Three spots of gulls enounce the anniversary in the sky;

   I am one to see,

I am supposed to listen

   like a lens;

off the point the gross ships steer beneath the rationale of bridges,

my photo sutures the idea of commerce

      to the brute economy of the calendar,

September is the doctrine I obey

of low sunlight on milky water;

the sky stalls, the valences sweep over the valley as vast shades,

soon the crude singe of the red paint on the red freighter,

      my clouds, these white conical heaps, this haze at the river's

western mouth, those accidental forms of debris on the shores, the island of reckless speech in the middle,

   the beaches that are the margins:

      my action is stuck between is and ought;

two gray smudges left,

arbitrary values

plummeting for fish

one veers

over the drowned trees of the bank;

Feeling does not precede experience

I need a correction

I have the paperback epics of the self

 on my back

I have the uniform mannerism of vapor, all else

  held to the shadows, some parts

the splendor of the best alabaster, but

  their sum

 (never mine)

a white river shell insists at the tip of my shoe

ARTIFICIAL

There is poison inside of the tattered weed

and the trash in the roadside ditch

generic birdmusic sourceless

(where?) I think in the brush the wet frogs

throat more of the same

with less derivation, rain

the asphalt beading oil, the washoff

moaning through a metal culvert;

I'll stop awhile and splurge;

plumes of dill ululate in the

sodium green breeze, the sidereal consumption

that void, the sky; do not defer from it

expend into it; I hear a faint frequency

in the clouds, near the speakers and

the hanging panels of a false ceiling

the noise is barely background

un-tapped desire is encoded there

all of the hype swallowed and gagged

it costs too much

and my resource is too small in the

spasming sumac bending

where the unseen source of music

plays and I let go finding it

I wanted to talk

Give it up, the voice said

   The voice

was the brief mediation between the self and the absorbing blank cliffs

there would be no talking, only listening to whomever this other

   that is the voice is

It's not so much the coarse melancholy, I said

Where was my sounding against it, in the ambient crash of water

and in its vicinity, effused starlight, the delicate stream realized into a

gorge over the past few thousand years, this was not a kind of

emptiness,

I will not delude myself

but then I did come along

and I waded upstream to the impassable falls, midnight, April,

the gap of night narrowed above me where rocks closed,

nebulae seared the overhang, all of the blue-white catastrophes

toned into the plummet, the spray blustering off of shale,

the ferns contorting, fronds in the wet air

This was not a place; this was an event:

I was measured by it—

little remained or time, but there was none other

to gauge besides me, remanded into what should be

forgotten (the stones would never remember)

    I wanted to be   not me

and there was   no other there

without me,   though I insisted in the falsity

no other was there——only the dispersal of

my own self

un-wildering where I went

ACTUARY

Now I have reread the ridgeline
  and used my citation,

I am not sure: centuries, chora of the forests, the cut of streams—

as ordered by their syllabic taxonomies;

they recorded   flowering dates
and rainfall,

their lost infancies followed into the hills, in the twilight

calamity-stars spun

and the catalog dropped
for a moment: see the disease:

    the x of matter & form,
the deadly catchall,

these are not two
but one category.

What else? I am attuned to the lodeline of bleached shells

radiating on a lateral rise to the south

(is this when the ledger fills with compact seas?) . . .

——   I made a copy of a rose,
  its blanched-blue luster pressed into the pages. . . . . . . broached,

  the inner operation of scent was
  snipped and trussed into the preserve.

There is a question.

An answer rises
planted in the clear-cut.

I had a concept,

      I edged on knees into a wreckage of limbs and was augmented
by little animals, lost pieces of paper, currencies penned on the walls
of *once*,

  there was a syllabic collision above my ears—— it sought the colloquial
way to say good lighting costs,

  and the clearance of all of it was the continuing epilogue to felled
poplars,

  came the sterling engines, now at work in the middle, making
tender lawns in every town, and the young yet dead leaves in the
tended, blue-green papery of a par under——

  these were questions of policy, these were *geologica*,

at the meeting they said hard water in the water system, as of yet——
they said several yeas and zoned self-sufficiency,

after, the fear arrived: the world was a tiny model,
I was cloistered within it, separate in my separateness——

one is so small in the age of terror as to be vast . . .
many devices are tuned to our choices . . .

I drove into the mountains
pines, groping at them, I
green air, I tried to breathe,
found a pale pillar of light,
was springing *find* and
dozers the clearing at the
mean *cul-de-sac*, and
always a freedom, but it is
neighbors, etc, in one con-
spreading branches taking
might contain all electric
grow onto the gray sky in total
another, the question asked is:
the 'trees' with? I am trying, I have
transparency of my self, it looks

and gravitated to the last
dry-heaved in the
I found a feather, I
in my innermost of
replace, the dust of
edge of the forest, I
the buyers know I is
good to have
figuration, the
shape in a form of the
flaring of thought, to
grotesque empathy, in
is there anything I can replace
a concept on a vellum
like a shut

gate— —it says the

has-been
and blood

is four-chambered
straining: clear it away.

Into the milkweed grove

where the green venture lusts up

the current shake-off   of dew late in the boom

of a dying season

though humming spectrum

though tending or orienting toward the hot

(hope) heyday   the surplus   here

with the spittled   lately homes

under a red umbra

a stream of chutes in the air

into an august cloud

the furious bluesky renewal of a go-on

and a monarch to-be

now in the toxic underthought

never meaning to   but do—

use the whole allotment

THE LAWS

The orphaned pocket of the wilderness
does not miss its connection
to the scheme of the rivers
or nurse trees

it declines where a sign
declares the boundary

The road to the sign was well worn
    The trail was clear
  I hiked through feral woods,
early winter, no more underbrush verve
The horned lark was
 in his evening singing
the vaunt of the last
western wave,
                a trumpet
pouring through the scenes

I broke out of the aspens into a meadow

In the center

The break-off
                    rock

                    focal in the grass
                    I rested my back
               against the face

the pan of the plains below me

a sacral lesion
or lichen
 deep in the granite

     seamed toward
 everything I could obscure there
by sitting there,

   no end to it,
it keeps on coming:

my primacy

If here
 were only unrealized
or only arrived at

in a meadow, biotic
without reason

you can't do this
you can't do that

but all spent beloveds are
stifled in the ache
and covered over

Each monster
will establish its own agenda

The errors rise collective from the pallid foreground

(as a streaming butchery)

some palms held out to witness

(some for applauding, to reinforce, or to authorize, to raise before the jury)

is it excessive enough

(is it deliberate and systematic)

ashen radiance after snow

(does it annihilate on a mass level)

what comes through

(stealing is the only originality)

wake up to recover

(or to not recover)

but if pin lights on the hill, if some edge of 3 am color

(listen, listen to a morning bird starting)

a moaning status against the rest

(in the off-peak hours)

no, the moment is not charged for

(this is an exemption to bring back to the others)

but there are still the hours to come

(and the accrual of the day to come)

and asking if that bird built a role

(on the slope or in the cottonwood)

or if in other forms of abstinence

(is not the question to ask anymore)

Vacant at first
a vessel to be filled

the flowerhead expelled
  into the autumn

and emanating through the fiery extremities of poplars

  I stood there in the mindless continuity of the season

From the viewing platform the wounds on the hillsides

were unseen, but a child chased a leaf

a, child, chasing, a, leaf,

collided with me on the stairs to the overlook, feigned

apology for that self-absorption

Cryphonectria parasitica

killed the chestnut forests

their spaces filled with trees
  whose buds in the spring

forget the prior extinctions

the crisis is too beautiful
but it is much uglier

they say new impervious hybrids

are "in the works"

GUIDELINE

I think it had
ruptured from questions

I should not have asked

  I keep to the path in the park, the leading, sequential green lights of
planning,

and off of this? the side streets, the same forms of ending radiance cuts
the blinds

onto the floor;

  how should I feel toward the slices of violence therein? the almanac is

in the wind, the ice is thinning on the plains, it is ceasing at the front
range, and in

  the summer, the new scars lay on the flat earth in the late morning
clarity;

the creek drains the oily parking lot, the buying eye scans past the
clutter

   lining the highway we dreamed these dreams against, properties at
the edge,

    the nail-scrape of this, communal masterpiece, the closeness of
the homes,

    the fences inconsequential barriers;

        Self-alteration is an easy transaction
of buying the very selves
we always wanted to be

even the books are bought

        And news?

the arguments arrive too far behind their source too late to our place
in the sprawl

the decisions made yesterday announced today, and the scratch
bled from the first,

the two voices narrating over the bodies within the footage

was an argument of if what was seen was genocide or piles;

We can't tell ourselves

from those whose loss is actual;

I was working on a grocery list, the broadcast was absorbed into four

sealed walls, the resonance met the space, the receiving area was

larger than itself,

a better value than

    I   would ever pay

    I   was thinking of the things

    I   thought

    I   needed

Some of these poems have appeared (or will soon appear), sometimes in different versions or with different titles, in the following publications:

"Harm" (as "Ten or Twelve Strokes of Havoc") in *Aphrodite of the Spangled Mind*. This poem invokes phrasing from Gerard Manley Hopkins' "Binsey Poplars."

"Was It/It Was," "Weapon Alpha" (as "Weapon Eclogue"), "Guideline," & "Two Reports" in *Columbia*.

"Tacit Rainbow" (as "Friend at the End") in *Five Fingers Review*. This poem is dedicated to Elizabeth Robinson.

"Bastion," "Rapier/Ravine" (as "Rapier"), & "Maverick" in *Interim*. "Rapier/ Ravine" adapts phrasing from witnesses testifying before a Congressional hearing on the Wounded Knee Massacre.

Parts of "Speaking For" (as "The Green Zone") in *Kulture Vulture*.

Parts of "Newness"(as " Patriot") & "Out of Lack" (as "The Future") in *La Fovea*. "Out of Lack" is dedicated to Andy Prall.

Parts of "Recovery Effort" and "Out of Lack" (as "Tracer") and parts of "Speaking For" (as "Chaparral"), "Eris," "Hellfire," & "Vulcan" in *Soft Targets*, V.1.1. and V.2.1. "Recovery Effort" is dedicated to Daniel Feinberg.

"Last of the Butterflies" (as "Super") as a broadside with Brian Teare's "What's" (titled "What's Super"), printed by *SOON Productions*.

Parts of "Rezone" as "Crotale," as an *Underwood Poetry* broadside.

"The Session" & "Rezone" in *Cordite Poetry Review* (Australia).

"Actuary" and "Species" in *Colorado Review*.

"Artificial" and "Annals" in *Electronic Poetry Review*.

"Misfits," "The Laws" (as "Nomos"), "Sale," "A Regime," and "A Spectacle" (as "Not Spectacle Enough") in *Gut Cult*.

Richard Greenfield was born in Southern California and spent much
of his childhood in the Pacific Northwest. He is the author of *A Carnage
in the Lovetrees* (University of California Press), which was listed as a
Top Ten University Press Book by BookSense in 2003. He is co-editor of
Apostrophe Books (www.apostrophebooks.org), a small press of poetry.